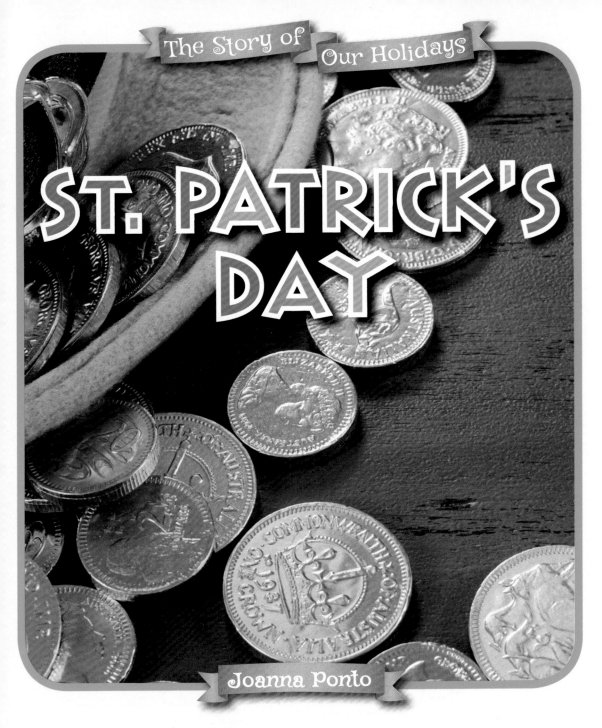

The Story of Our Holidays

ST. PATRICK'S DAY

Joanna Ponto

Enslow Publishing
101 W. 23rd Street
Suite 240
New York, NY 10011
USA

enslow.com

Published in 2016 by Enslow Publishing, LLC.
101 W. 23rd Street, Suite 240, New York, NY 10011

Library of Congress Cataloging-in-Publication Data

Ponto, Joanna.
   St. Patrick's day / Joanna Ponto.
      pages cm. — (The story of our holidays)
   Includes bibliographical references and index.
   ISBN 978-0-7660-7461-3 (library binding)
   ISBN 978-0-7660-7473-6 (pbk.)
   ISBN 978-0-7660-7467-5 (6-pack)
   1. Saint Patrick's Day—Juvenile literature. I. Title.
   GT4995.P3P66 2015
   394.262—dc23

                         2015031042

Printed in the United States of America

To Our Readers: We have done our best to make sure all website addresses in this book were active and appropriate when we went to press. However, the author and the publisher have no control over and assume no liability for the material available on those websites or on any websites they may link to. Any comments or suggestions can be sent by e-mail to customerservice@enslow.com.

Portions of this book originally appeared in the book *St. Patrick's Day: Parades, Shamrocks, and Leprechauns.*

Photos Credits: Cover, p. 1 Milleflore Images/Shutterstock.com; p. 4 Thomas Barrat/Shutterstock.com; p. 6 lynx_v/Shutterstock.com; p. 7 Allison Joyce/Getty Images News/Getty Images; p. 9 jordache/Shutterstock.com; pp. 11, 16 Private Collection/© Look and Learn/Bridgeman Images; p. 15 H. Armstrong Roberts/ClassicStock/Getty Images; p. 18 Private Collection/The Stapleton Collection/Bridgeman Images;. p. 22 HelenStock/Shutterstock; p. 24 Silver Spiral Arts/Shutterstock.com; p. 26 © AP Images; p. 28 Timothy A. Clary/AFP/Getty Images; p. 29 Leelu/Shutterstock.com; p. 31 Karen Huang.

Contents

The Chicago River is turned green every year on March 17 to celebrate St. Patrick's Day.

Chapter 1

A Green Day

Every year on March 17, lots of people and places get out their green. Classrooms and businesses are decorated in green. School cafeterias serve green Jell-O. Bakeries sell green cupcakes. In Chicago, Illinois, green dye is put into the Chicago River to turn the water green for a day. March 17 is Saint Patrick's Day. It is an Irish holiday and a day for many people to wear the color green.

Ireland

Ireland is a country in Europe. It has miles of green fields and valleys. Ireland even has a special name. It is known as the Emerald Isle. Emeralds are beautiful bright green jewels.

The Tricolor

The national flag of Ireland is called the Tricolor. The orange part stands for one of the major religious groups of Ireland, the Protestants. The green part stands for the other major religious group, the Irish Catholics. And the white part stands for peace between the people of both religions.

The Irish celebrate St. Patrick's Day every year. St. Patrick is Ireland's patron saint. A patron saint watches over people and places and keeps them safe. The Irish people believe not only that St. Patrick protects them, but also that he brought the Christian religion to Ireland.

Ireland is a small island nation west of the United Kingdom.

Green All Over

St. Patrick's Day is celebrated outside of Ireland, too. There are St. Patrick's Day celebrations wherever Irish people live, including in the United States.

In many ways, St. Patrick's Day has become an American

holiday. It is not celebrated throughout the country. It is not an official government holiday like Presidents' Day. Schools, banks, and businesses are all open on St. Patrick's Day. The mail is delivered, too. But everyone is welcome to celebrate St. Patrick's Day. Even people who are not Irish can enjoy it. March 17 is a day for parades, parties, and having fun. So on St. Patrick's Day, put on something green and join the fun!

Parades are a popular way to celebrate St. Patrick's Day.

Chapter 2

The Story of Saint Patrick

St. Patrick's Day is based on a man who was not Irish, even though it is an Irish holiday. His name wasn't even Patrick!

St. Patrick was born somewhere in the British Isles, the area that includes England, Scotland, and Wales. Yet St. Patrick was not British, either. He was probably born in the year 385. At that time, people from Rome, Italy, ruled the land. So Patrick grew up as a Roman.

Young Patrick

Not much is known about Patrick's childhood. His name was probably Maewyn Succat, and his father was an important worker in the Roman government. Their family had a lot of money and servants, and they lived in a large house by the sea.

As a boy, Patrick did not seem saintly. He did not pray all the time or always listen to the priests. However, that all changed when trouble started in Ireland, which was called Hibernia.

Fierce fighting tribes lived in Hibernia. The men of these tribes often crossed the sea to raid the British Isles. They stole things, took people hostage, and sold the captives as slaves in Hibernia.

The Famous Irish Church

Dublin, Ireland, is home to one of the largest—and most famous—churches in the country. St. Patrick's Cathedral was built in 1191, and in 1320, it became Ireland's first university. Many people visit the cathedral every year to pray and learn about the history of this special church.

There is also a St. Patrick's Cathedral in New York City. It is a beautiful church that is found among the towering skyscrapers in Manhattan.

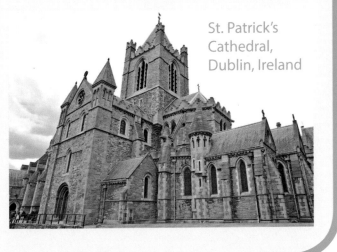

St. Patrick's Cathedral, Dublin, Ireland

When he was just sixteen, Patrick was kidnapped by raiders from Hibernia. Some of his family's servants were taken, too. A powerful chief named Miliuc bought Patrick to Hibernia to be his slave.

Miliuc owned many sheep. Patrick became a shepherd and made sure the animals did not run away. He watched over his master's sheep and lived outside with them.

It was a hard life. There were many cold and rainy nights. Patrick felt lonely and sad. He thought he might have been captured because God was punishing him. He wished he had listened to the priests.

Patrick was a shepherd for six years. During that time, he became very religious. He prayed often, and he began to have visions. He believed God was appearing before him and speaking to him.

A Voice in the Night

One night, Patrick heard a voice that brought welcome news. The voice told Patrick a ship would take him home soon. Patrick was far from the sea. It was dangerous for him to try to go there. A slave who ran away could be killed. But Patrick believed God wanted him to go.

Patrick traveled more than two hundred miles. Finally, he reached the sea, where he found a ship waiting for him. At first, the ship's

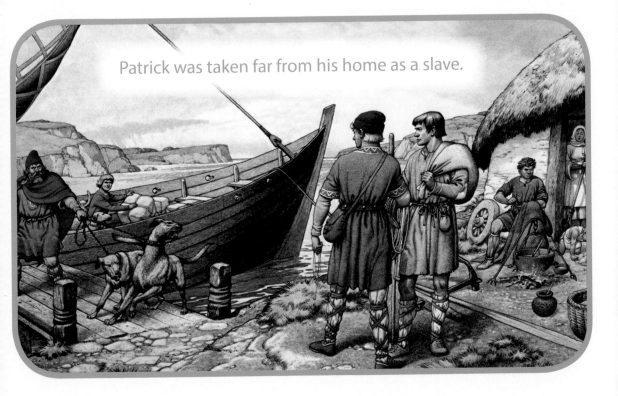

Patrick was taken far from his home as a slave.

captain would not help Patrick since he was a runaway slave. The captain could be punished if he was caught helping a runaway slave.

Patrick left, but he did not know what to do next. So, he began to pray. Perhaps Patrick's prayers were heard. People on the ship called out to and told him to come back. The captain changed his mind.

Patrick wanted to go home. But that did not happen. There were storms at sea, and the ship crashed. The men ended up in a place that seemed to be deserted. There was no food in sight. It looked like they might die from hunger. Nearly a month passed, and the men grew weak.

Patrick asked God to save them. He also prayed for food. Before long, the men spotted a herd of wild pigs. No one knew where the pigs came from. But the captain thought that Patrick's prayers had been answered. The men caught some of the pigs. They now had food and would not starve.

No one really knows what happened after that. Patrick later wrote that he became a slave again. No one knows for sure who captured him. Some people say a group of fighting men found the ship's crew and all the men except Patrick were sold as slaves. The story says that the group of fighting men kept Patrick with them.

Another Ending

There is another story about the ship's captain. The captain believed in Patrick. He had seen him pray for food. The captain never wanted to be hungry again. So he forced Patrick to stay close.

We do not know which story is true. But Patrick was not a slave for very long. Once again, he heard a voice. This time, the voice said that Patrick would be free in two months. And he was!

Chapter 3

Priest Patrick

Free at last, Patrick was sure of what his next step should be. When he was a slave, he had not been allowed to go to school. Now he wanted to study religion. Patrick went to France and learned all he could. He became a priest.

In the year 432, Patrick was made a bishop. This is an important position in the Catholic Church. The pope is the head of the Catholic Church. He gave the new bishop the name Patricius, Latin for Patrick.

Back to Ireland

Patrick returned to his homeland. He had been gone for many years. His family was happy to see him. But he did not stay home for long. Patrick believed God wanted him to go back to Ireland.

A Famous Rock

Blarney is a village in Ireland that is famous for a stone at the very top of Blarney Castle. Irish people believe that the power of Gaelic gab (speaking) is given to those who kiss the Blarney Stone.

Patrick wanted the Irish to love God. He hoped that they would become Christians. Patrick gathered together a group of priests. They set sail for Ireland. It would be the most important trip of Patrick's life.

Druids

People in Ireland had many different beliefs. They prayed to many gods. Magic was part of their religion, too. Many different chiefs ruled over Ireland. Each chief had his own religious advisers. They were known as Druids.

Druids prayed to different gods of nature. They held secret ceremonies in oak forests. Druids were thought to have strong magical powers. People believed Druids could see the future. Druids made life difficult for Patrick. They thought he was their enemy. They said that Patrick was evil. They even tried to kill him.

Saint Patrick

Patrick would not leave Ireland. He wanted people to become Christians and love God. He built churches and started Christian schools. He also traveled throughout the country. Patrick talked to the people. He spoke to their chiefs, too. He told them about his religion and shared his love for God. Patrick refused to give up. He remained in Ireland for more than thirty years. In time, some of the chiefs began to believe in Patrick and his faith. The chiefs and their followers became

Nature was very special to the Druids. Here, a group of Druids performs a ritual celebrating trees and the forest.

Christians. They felt his kindness, and they began to believe his words.

Patrick did what he had hoped to do. He helped thousands of Irish people find God. He helped turn Ireland into a Christian land.

Patrick died on March 17 in the year 461. After his death, the Church made him a saint. A saint is someone who is officially recognized by the Church for their holiness.

St. Patrick used the shamrock to teach pagans about the Holy Trinity.

We celebrate St. Patrick's Day on the anniversary of Patrick's death. In Ireland, it is a religious holiday. People honor St. Patrick by going to special church services. They also enjoy getting together with family and friends.

Chapter 4

Stories and Symbols of the Saint

Over time many stories, or legends, have been written and told about this saint. One St. Patrick's Day legend is about snakes. It says that St. Patrick cast a spell over the snakes of Ireland. Some people say he beat a drum to frighten the snakes. Then the snakes crawled into the sea. Ireland was free from snakes forever.

The Legend of the Shamrock

Another St. Patrick's Day legend is about shamrocks. A shamrock is a small green plant with three leaves. It looks like a clover. St. Patrick used the three leaves of the shamrock to teach people in Ireland about the Holy Trinity. The shamrock's three leaves are part of the same plant. The Father, the Son,

St. Patrick often preached to the Irish people about the teachings of the Christian faith.

and the Holy Spirit are all part of one God. The shamrock became a symbol of St. Patrick and a symbol of Ireland.

Fairies and Leprechauns

Irish fairies and leprechauns are also symbols of St. Patrick's Day. Both were believed to be small magical spirits. Druids had believed in magic. But St. Patrick's teachings made these things less important. In stories, the spirits became smaller in size, too. People spoke of the magic of the little people or wee folk.

Irish fairies are supposed to love to dance. Stories say they twirled and whirled all day and wore out their shoes. People believed that there were also little men who mended the fairies' shoes. They dressed in green, wore cocked hats and leather aprons, and carried tools for fixing shoes. They were leprechauns.

Lucky Clover

People believe that it is lucky to find a four-leaf clover. They also believe that the leaves have special meanings. The first leaf stands for faith. The second leaf stands for hope. The third leaf stands for love. The fourth leaf stands for luck.

Leprechauns worked at night repairing shoes while the fairies slept. The fairies left gold coins for the leprechauns to pay them for their work. The leprechauns carefully saved their coins. Stories say they had large pots filled with all their gold coins.

Irish stories were often told with music. Sometimes people would play a harp, a stringed instrument that has a pleasing tone. The harp is one of Ireland's oldest instruments. It has also become a symbol of Ireland.

Symbols of the Saint

On St. Patrick's Day, we see many symbols. Harps are played. Children hear stories about leprechauns and Irish fairies.

When people wear green it is called the wearing of the green. The color reminds us of the shamrock. On March 17, the spirit of Ireland comes alive. We know it is St. Patrick's Day.

Chapter 5

Celebrating the Saint

The first U.S. celebration of St. Patrick's Day happened a long time ago. In the 1700s, many people from Ireland came to America hoping to start a better life. They had celebrated St. Patrick's Day in Ireland. They did the same in their new country, the United States.

St. Patrick's Parades

The first official St. Patrick's Day celebration in the United States was in Boston, Massachusetts, in 1737. Many Irish people settled there. They had a St. Patrick's Day parade.

St. Patrick's Day parades are common today. More than 120 cities in the United States have them. The largest parade is in

Boston, Massachusetts, holds a big St. Patrick's Day parade with floats like this one. Some kids dress up in costumes.

New York City. But Chicago, Illinois, and Philadelphia, Pennsylvania, also have big parades.

St. Patrick's Day parades are exciting. High school bands play, and sometimes there are clowns and horses. Children dressed as leprechauns and fairies may march in the parade.

Often people from Irish clubs are in the parade. Many people wear green costumes. They might pass out green flowers to the people watching.

Everyone comes out to cheer and watch the people in the parade. They might wave small Irish flags or twirl long green ribbons. Children hold onto green balloons. Everyone claps when their favorite band passes.

In Manchester, New Hampshire, it is easy to figure out where the parade starts. A giant shamrock is painted on that spot. Marchers in the St. Patrick's Day parade in Milwaukee, Wisconsin, always enjoy the view. Businesses along the parade route decorate their windows. There is even a contest for the best decorated window. Judges pick the winner before the parade begins.

School Celebrations

Parades are great. But there are also other things to enjoy on St. Patrick's Day. Many schools celebrate the holiday. Children often make green decorations. They might hang up paper shamrocks and leprechaun hats. Sometimes there are St. Patrick's Day parties. Green cupcakes and cookies are always popular. Chocolate coins in gold foil are fun, too. These look like gold from a leprechaun's pot.

Some schools have special St. Patrick's Day activities. An Irish storyteller may be invited. Sometimes Irish dancers perform. St.

Patrick's Day contests are fun, too. There may be a contest for the best St. Patrick's Day poster. A prize might also go to the boy or girl wearing the most green.

Heart, Hands, and Crown

Claddagh rings date back hundreds of years. In the 1600s, they were often exchanged by friends or lovers. Each of the ring's three parts have special meanings. The heart stands for love. The hands stand for faith and friendship. The crown stands for loyalty.

Irish Fairs and Festivals

St. Patrick's Day festivals are held all over the United States. There is always Irish music. You can see Irish dancers, too. Some are local dance groups. Others come from Ireland for the festival.

All sorts of Irish crafts may be put on display. Sometimes people watch the crafts being made. Irish glassblowers make vases. Irish silversmiths work with silver to make rings and bracelets. Often the jewelry has Irish symbols on it.

Beauty contests are also part of many St. Patrick's Day festivals. The winner is named the festival queen. She will wear a crown and sit on a special throne. Her title may be Miss Shamrock or Miss Irish Rose.

The festivals always have special children's events. There are St. Patrick's Day puppet shows. Young people also learn old Irish songs. Often they can watch sheepdogs at work. Sheepdogs are important in Ireland. They keep the sheep together in the fields.

The Irish Fair in St. Paul, Minnesota, is a large event. It is a two-day celebration. Thousands of people attend. For them, it is a great way to enjoy St. Patrick's Day.

Other people choose athletic events to celebrate the holiday. They may sign up for St. Patrick's Day races. One St. Patrick's Day race is held in Colorado Springs, Colorado. Nearly five hundred runners take part. Afterward there is a one-mile race for children. All the young runners get prizes.

New York City has the country's biggest St. Patrick's Day parade. It also has one of the nation's biggest buildings, the Empire State Building. On St. Patrick's Day the Empire State Building is lit up in green. This famous skyscraper has a special tie to St. Patrick. Construction on it began on March 17, 1930. Many of the workers there were Irish. They were especially proud that they were working

The Empire State Building goes green for St. Patrick's Day!

on this terrific building and that the work was starting on St. Patrick's Day.

Festive Foods

St. Patrick's Day can be fun anywhere. In many cities, water fountains spray green water. Irish clubs have St. Patrick's Day breakfasts. They even serve green pancakes.

Restaurants also have special St. Patrick's Day menus. They serve tasty Irish dishes, such as corned beef and cabbage, shepherd's pie, and Irish stew.

Many families get together for the holiday. They may share a meal or sing Irish songs. St. Patrick's Day is a more religious holiday in Ireland than it is in the United States. But some people in the United States also go to church then. Churches often offer special St. Patrick's Day services.

On his holiday, Irish people remember St. Patrick and celebrate being Irish. But everyone can enjoy the festivities on St. Patrick's Day.

St. Patrick's Day Shepherd's Pie*

Ingredients:

1 pound (450 g) ground beef, turkey, or lamb

1 medium onion, diced

2 cloves garlic, minced

1 teaspoon (5 mL) black pepper

1 teaspoon (5 mL) Italian seasoning (or a pinch each of dried oregano, rosemary, and basil)

1 tablespoon (15 mL) Worcestershire sauce

2 tablespoons (15 g) all-purpose flour

½ cup (120 mL) chicken, beef, or vegetable stock.

5 large potatoes, diced and peeled

1½ cups (225 g) frozen green peas and carrots

3 tablespoons (45 g) butter

salt

Directions:

1. In a medium pot, bring 2 quarts of water to a boil. Add salt and potatoes. Cook until soft, about 15 to 18 minutes.

2. Meanwhile, in a medium skillet, add ground beef, onions, and garlic. Cook until the meat is brown and the onions turn translucent. Add seasonings and Worcestershire sauce.

3. Stir in flour until well combined. Let cook for about two minutes, until the meat drippings are thick.

4. Add stock and vegetables, reduce heat to simmer. Cook for approximately 5 minutes, until thick.

5. Prepare an oven-safe casserole dish by spraying it with nonstick cooking spray. Carefully place beef mixture in the bottom.

6. Preheat oven to 350°F (175°C).

7. Drain potatoes carefully. The water could still be extremely hot!

8. Using a potato smasher or a large spoon, smash the potatoes slightly. You want them to be squished, but still in large pieces.

9. Spoon the potatoes on top of the beef mixture, covering the meat and vegetables completely.

10. Divide the butter into small pats and place evenly over the potatoes. Sprinkle with salt and pepper to taste.

11. Bake in the oven for about 25 to 30 minutes, or until the potatoes are gold in color and the beef and vegetables are bubbling.

* Adult supervision required.

St. Patrick's Day Craft

You can have your own St. Patrick's Day treasure!

Here are the supplies you will need:

2-inch (5-centimeter) Dixie cup

strip of black construction paper, 2 inches (5 centimeters) wide and 6 inches (15 centimeters) long

20 pebbles or 10 small stones

gold magic marker or paint

thin piece of green ribbon, 8 inches (20 centimeters) long

glue or tape

Directions:

1. Wrap the construction paper around the cup. Glue or tape the ends together. This is your pot for the gold.

2. Color each pebble with the gold magic marker or paint. These are your gold pieces.

3. Place the pebbles in the cup.

4. Tie a ribbon around the cup to add a touch of St. Patrick's Day green.

Leprechaun's Pot of Gold

*Safety Note: Be sure to ask for help from an adult, if needed, to complete this project.

Glossary

bishop—An important person in some Christian churches.

Druids—Religious advisers or priests in ancient Ireland.

emerald—A bright green precious jewel.

Hibernia—The name for ancient Ireland.

leprechaun—A small magical make-believe man. Stories said that leprechauns mended fairy shoes and had pots of gold.

patron saint—A saint who watches over and protects people and things.

shamrock—A small green plant with three leaves.

shepherd—A person who keeps the sheep together in the fields.

symbol—Something that stands for something else.

vision—Something seen in a dream.

Learn More

Books

Bevendes, Mary. *St. Patrick's Day Shamrocks*. Mankato, MN: Child's World, 2015.

Keogh, Josie. *St. Patrick's Day*. New York: PowerKids Press, 2013.

Lindeen, Mary. *St. Patrick's Day* (Beginning-To-Read). Chicago: Norwood House Press, 2015.

Owen, Ruth. *St. Patrick's Day Origami*. New York: Rosen Publishing Group, 2014.

Websites

St. Patrick's Day: March 17th
wilstar.com/holidays/patrick.htm
Head to this site to learn about the history and customs of St. Patrick's Day.

St. Patrick's Day
saint-patrick.com/history.htm
Check out this site for the history of Saint Patrick.

St. Patrick's Day
fun.familyeducation.com/st.-patricks-day/holidays/32935.html
Learn all about Ireland with games, recipes, and a whole lot more.

Index